"With practical advice and down-to-earth w....., those who are desiring to truly make good choices to succeed. This is a compelling and powerful tool and should be placed in the hands of everyone who needs a little push on the road to high achievement. Ms. Drossner's *IWoWs* will make a wonderful, life-altering gift and a treasure to pass on to others."

—Vickie Watts, book reviewer at vicklea.com and retired teacher

"Imagine being able to change unproductive mental habits, set and meet high expectations, and unlock hidden potential. Amy Drossner presents a clear and easy strategy to inspire readers of all ages to new levels of productivity and positivity in her entertaining book."

—Dana Mentink, *USA Today* bestselling author and retired teacher

"We strive to develop in all of our young people characteristics of strong work ethic, integrity, and having a growth mindset. The tips, strategies, and advice in *IWoWs* provide a strong framework to guide learners through the development of these important life-ready skills."

—Chris Martinez, high school principal and teacher of eighteen years

"Amy Drossner has created a clear and concise set of life lessons that can help anyone be more successful. This book shines with hard-earned wisdom and is written in consumable, short chapters that build to a cohesive philosophy of empowerment and personal ownership. I'd highly recommend this to anyone to keep on hand and reference regularly!"

—Michael Laurence Turner, MBSS, ME, PhD, and author of research articles published by *Science Education* and the American Evaluation Association

"Tried and true advice handed down through the ages and updated for Generation Z and Generation Alpha. This book is easy to read, easy to understand, and to the point, but also has enough amplification to drive the point home."

—Mark Dotson, university research scientist, retired military officer and instructor, father, and youth Sunday school teacher

IWoWs

INFINITE WORDS OF WISDOM

— OR —

I WOW THEM WITH

INFINITE WORDS OF WISDOM

A collection of sage advice from a classroom teacher for ~~her students~~ *everyone*

AMY DROSSNER

ABD

ISBN: 979-8-218-18649-4
Library of Congress Control Number: 2023906931

Printed in the United States of America

To my dad, who taught me the incredible power of thought relative to action, and who is the foundation for each IWoW in this book.

"How can I learn to do the right thing at the right time? Who are the people I most need, and to whom should I, therefore, pay more attention than to the rest? And, what affairs are the most important and need my first attention?"

—Leo Tolstoy, *The Three Questions*

INTRODUCTION

When I started my journey as a public school teacher, I had no idea what I was getting into. Literally no idea. I did not prepare to be a schoolteacher, and it had never crossed my mind that becoming a schoolteacher would be an option as a career. I was more of a worldly, large-scale, global-minded, international travel and business kind of person. But at the time, I needed a job. I knew someone who knew someone, and then I was in an interview and a classroom faster than I could take a breath.

Fast forward, twenty-eight years later, and I am still in that classroom, a little wiser, much more capable and knowledgeable, and a whole lot less naive. The little collection of wisdom presented here began as a simple list of pieces of advice that I found myself repeating to students quite regularly. One day I realized that I tended to say the same phrases and give the same advice to students on any given day, so I decided to start writing them down. Initially there were only three or four of them. But as I continued my journey, and five years of teaching became twelve, then fifteen, then twenty-five, and now twenty-eight and beyond, and as generations of students have come and gone, I've developed more Words of Wisdom and added more and more to this list.

I like to think that I was impacting the students with these Words of Wisdom in some profound way—that I was wowing them, inspiring them to seek greatness, persevere, be instilled with integrity, and have an incredible work ethic in all that they do. I truly want to believe this was my impact. The reality probably was that their eyerolls were about as much reaction and result as I was going to get, along with the occasional pushback and resistance at accepting these Words of Wisdom as truly helpful and not just some blathering inspirational nonsense. I realized after a while that these Words of Wisdom were mostly about changing established mental habits, which is one of the most difficult things for humans—especially stubborn teenagers—to train their brains to do. However, I do believe that these Words of Wisdom, or IWoWs as I like to call them (Infinite Words of Wisdom, or I *wow* them with my Infinite Words of Wisdom), are an important guide not only for school and academics, but also for life's journey. There is no time or age limit or defined context to these IWoWs. Although they came into being within the context of a high school environment and schoolwork in general, these Words of Wisdom can just as easily apply to other real-world situations, in any context, at any age. Take these IWoWs to heart now, at whatever age you currently are and in whatever situation you find yourself, and they will stay with you as a powerful influence over your mental habits, the decisions you make, and the trajectory of your life's journey.

Hello, and welcome to the rest of your life. Today is day one.

NOBODY RISES TO
LOW EXPECTATIONS.

I wish I could take credit for this tenet. A presenter at a conference I was attending many years ago mentioned this phrase in his speech, and while I admit I do not remember the surrounding context of that speech, this one phrase has profoundly impacted my teaching philosophy ever since. It has definitely been my mantra and guiding principle in the classroom. Most, if not all, of my IWoWs fall under the umbrella of this philosophy.

Your classroom teachers, band directors, tutors, coaches, mentors, and anyone charged with educating you are there to challenge you, get you to expand your skill set, and build up your knowledge. Do not resent them for it. Why would you waste energy on such a negative mentality? Use your mental energy for a more positive outcome. Keep in mind the ultimate objective of why you are there under their supervision to begin with. Don't fight it. Accept that these people are there to educate you, and your job is to learn something. So, every single day, decide to learn something.

To help my students with this daily decision and develop an innate expectation of high-quality work, I consistently remind them to be in the habit of going above and beyond the bare minimum when completing tasks. I created an acronym,

DECIDE, to help them with creating quality components and content. This acronym could easily apply to any type of work process:

Details: Describe with details and descriptive language.
Elaborate: Elaborate on your ideas with supporting details.
Create: Create unique content with what you've learned.
Imagine: Inform using imaginative, original details.
Define: Define problems; offer solutions or alternatives.
Explain: Explain with details to ensure understanding.

Before beginning any task, ask yourself, "Will I DECIDE to apply the recommended strategies in order to meet expectations of high-quality work?" Before considering any task to be complete, ask yourself, "Did I DECIDE to meet expectations of high-quality work?" The strategies imbedded in the DECIDE acronym are not exclusive to a school environment or academic work. In an office setting, fieldwork setting, or even if you are alone working on a home project or a hobby, expect high expectations everywhere you go and in everything you do, especially for yourself. Decide to rise to challenges. Face them head on. Decide to learn something. Don't walk away, give in, or give up just because something is difficult, different, or complex. If you consistently refuse to face a challenge and work your way through something that is more difficult than you would like or are accustomed to, you will never rise above the level where you currently are. You will never make progress, you will never improve, and you will be stuck for eternity at your current level of ability and skill. How utterly boring. There will come a time in life when you'll ask yourself, "Is this it? There must be more." There is absolutely more. There is so, so much more, but you cannot passively wait for it to come to you. You have to accept that there is no magical moment when it all suddenly appears on its own. That won't ever happen. You have to decide to seek it out and allow yourself access to it. It will take hard work, dedication, perseverance, and mental effort to move to the next level.

DO NOT ALLOW YOURSELF TO BE MENTALLY LAZY.

You must train yourself not to be mentally lazy. Never, ever, ever say, "I don't know," without even thinking about a possible answer or solution first. How do you know that you don't know? You may not remember something at the exact moment you are asked to produce it, but if you pause to think about a solution, process the information, and search through your bank of resources and learned or acquired content, chances are that you actually do have the answer.

And yes, it is perfectly okay to pause. In this paperless, digital world of screens and virtual buttons and clicks, it is very easy to become accustomed to finding a quick, instantaneous answer. But not everything can be instantaneous. Many things, in order to truly learn them, require a mental process on your part. Take a moment to think, process, make your brain work, and dive deep into the database of knowledge that is within your mental grasp.

And in the entirely possible event that you truly do not know (meaning that the information is not in your mental or tangible database), refer to the opening IWoW about rising to the challenge. View this as an opportunity to learn something. Instead of saying, "I don't know," and then moving on or walking away, change your mental habits to say, "I don't know, but I will find out." And then go and seek out the information. Seek knowledge. Learn something. Always be in the habit of learning something. This is how you strengthen your mentality and raise your own personal bar. Rise to a challenge, meet the challenge, move the bar, and seek out the next challenge.

ALWAYS STRIVE FOR PERFECTION, BUT NEVER EXPECT TO ACHIEVE IT.

Perfection is so incredibly subjective. It cannot be defined, at least not in any official capacity. If you expect to achieve perfection, you will perpetually be disappointed. If you believe that you've achieved it, you'll stop trying to improve. However, if you continue working diligently towards perfection without any expectation of achieving it, your progress will be infinite. You'll continue to learn, and your intellect will continue to grow and develop in perpetuity.

Anything you do, whether it be academic, scholastic, or something routinely quotidian, no matter how good or well done you believe it to be, can always be better. Progress is based on practice, effort, making honest mistakes, learning from them, improving, and moving forward. We learn as we go. Any academic piece or final product is a representation of the quality of work that you put into each individual part. An essay you write, a portrait you paint, a speech you prepare and deliver—every step of the process, everything you do, matters and has importance in the overall whole picture of your collective efforts. Honest mistakes are part of this process, and you must accept that you will make mistakes along the way and use them to learn, improve, and make progress.

You may be asking, "Well then, at what point is something considered 'finished?' What is the end point of any piece of work if it can't be considered finished, perfect, and ready to go?" You have to make that decision. Usually, your instinct will tell you if a final product is finished and ready to go. You are your own worst critic, and while people do tend to be hard on themselves, there are times when your own criticisms are pretty accurate. You know that nagging feeling you have about a homework assignment, presentation, or essay after you write the last few words or answer the last question? Pay attention to that feeling. Sure, sometimes it truly is uncertainty about your answer or information being correct or not. But just as likely, it could be your own instinct telling you, "Hey, this thing could be better," which is why you should continuously strive for perfection, even if it cannot be attained. You should always seek out knowledge and aim for achievement more than perfection. Knowledge can be quantified, and achievement can be measured and recognized. Perfection has no parameters and cannot be defined.

HONEST MISTAKES
INDICATE HONEST EFFORT.

Please notice that I specify *honest* mistakes and *honest* effort. We are talking about mistakes that result from honest, true effort that have a foundation rooted in integrity and sincerity. While it is completely normal to feel apprehension and nervousness about making a mistake or doing something incorrectly, you should not consider committing an honest mistake as an obstacle or prohibiting factor. It is perfectly okay to fear these mistakes, but you should also accept the fact that they will naturally occur as part of an honest process where you are trying to learn something new or different.

Everything is new, until it isn't. At one point in your life, every single thing that you currently know how to do, know about, have information on—everything—was new and different. You learned all of it, with guaranteed mistakes along the way. Imagine if you avoided doing any of those things just because you were afraid of making a mistake. You wouldn't know how to play a sport, build a birdhouse, dance, make cookies, play an instrument, speak intelligently, draw a picture—you wouldn't even be able to walk if you avoided the possibility of falling down. This is the epitome and the symbolism of the lesson learned from mistakes. You fall down six times, but you do not stay down. You get up a seventh time and try again.

Whether in class, practice, training, or work, there is no progress made if you choose to avoid a particular task because you are afraid you will make a mistake. If you attempt the task with honest effort and do make a mistake, that means that you are making an effort based on integrity, and you know what you need to work on in order to improve.

Choosing to cheat or plagiarize with the goal being to avoid making a mistake . . . well, cheating or plagiarizing is an egregious mistake in and of itself. You will not learn anything new, and you will not make progress. This type of mistake is most definitely not rooted in honesty, integrity, or sincerity.

DON'T FOCUS ON WHAT YOU DON'T KNOW. FOCUS ON WHAT YOU DO KNOW.

Integrity is everything. Your teacher, manager, boss, supervisor, coach—anyone higher up than you—always wants to see honest work and honest effort from you, and they provide you with opportunities to do so. When you present work that isn't yours, you have cheated. You have eliminated all possibility of proving what you—YOU—can do. You have obliterated any trust and faith that has been bestowed upon you—and after betraying that trust and faith, it will be very difficult to earn them back.

"How else can I say what I don't know how to say?"

Why would you even try to? Your teacher, manager, or supervisor isn't asking you to demonstrate what you don't know. You are being asked to show what you DO know—what you have learned based on your lessons, training, and/or studies.

"How can I do what I don't know how to do?"

This isn't even possible. You can only do what you DO know how to do, what you have been taught, have learned, and have studied or trained for.

"How else can I write what I don't know how to write?"

Please. We can go on and on. I have some possibly surprising news for you: your higher-ups don't want you to show them what you don't know. They don't want you to do what you don't know how to do or write what you don't know how to write. It is completely illogical, irrational, and unfair to expect you to perform or produce work that you haven't learned how to produce.

Your teachers, supervisors, and coaches want you to show them what you have learned. They want you to show them how you can apply what they have taught you. They are not interested in what you don't know or can't do. They are there to teach, train, and show you the way. Your task is simple: demonstrate to them that you have learned and can apply what they have worked so hard to teach you in a variety of real-world contexts.

Integrity is everything. No matter where you are in life, it is never too late to instill integrity into everything you do. Start now.

A ZERO GRADE IS THE WORST KIND OF BAD GRADE YOU CAN EARN AND THE EASIEST KIND OF BAD GRADE TO AVOID.

This one is so incredibly easy. Just. Do. The. Work. It really is that simple. A zero grade shows absolutely zero effort. Whether you earned a zero grade for not doing and turning in the work or for plagiarizing something or someone else's work, the result is the same: a zero grade for zero effort. This is truly the worst kind of bad grade you could possibly earn. You are turning in literally zero effort. That is horrible and even a bit shameful.

Doing honest work on an assignment, turning it in, and getting everything one hundred percent incorrect would be better than plagiarizing or doing nothing at all since it at least shows that an honest effort was made. In these cases, teachers would consult with you, ensure that you understand, and probably even give you a second chance on the assignment.

This is why the zero grade is the absolute worst kind of bad grade you could earn, and the easiest kind of bad grade to avoid. Just do the work. Turn it in. Repeat. And as you are doing the work, keep in mind some of the other IWoWs. Rise to the challenge. Move the bar. Don't allow yourself to be mentally lazy. Seek knowledge. Learn something.

YOU HAVE TO WORK FOR WHAT YOU WANT, EVEN IF YOU DON'T WANT IT.

I know, it seems contradictory. There are some things that we are required to do to reach a desirable outcome. Often, we want the outcome, but not the work involved in order to make that outcome a reality. Or, just as frequently, we really don't want a particular outcome, but it may be required as a necessary step to achieve a long-term goal. For example, you really, truly, do not want to take a music composition class, but you also realize that it is a required part of becoming a better musician. You really don't want to run that mile today, but you know it is a necessary part of becoming a better athlete. You really, seriously do not want to take a certain course in school or a training seminar at work, but you know that it is a requirement to earn the diploma or promotion that you want.

You want the end result without going through the work of making it a reality. Life doesn't work that way. If you want the outcome badly enough, you will do the work to make it happen, even if you don't particularly like the necessary steps along the way. Always keep in mind:

You don't have to like it. You just have to do what you need to do to get through it.

Many things in life just suck. Seriously. The tasks you're asked to do, the classes you're required to take, the people you're assigned to work with on a group project, the guy you don't want to talk to but need a signature from—life is chock-full of things you don't want to do. But the mentality of, "I don't like this; therefore, I choose not to do it," will not get you very far at all in the real world.

There is no policy sheet, set of rules, syllabus, or regulation in existence anywhere that says, "You are required to like this." You're in a requisite class you don't like, a practice session you don't want to be in, a seminar you don't want to attend. It is perfectly okay to not like any particular part of the process along the path to your ultimate goal. You do not have to like it, nor are you required to. You just have to get through, finish, and move on to being that much closer to your goal.

No one will penalize, judge, or discipline you for simply not liking something that is a required part of your process. Someone probably will penalize, judge, or discipline you if you act on your dislike by refusing to meet the requirements of a requisite course, not attending a mandatory seminar, not completing a task, or skipping practice. This is a choice that you make: either suck it up, do what you have to do to the best of your ability with integrity, and move towards your ultimate goal, or don't do what you have to do, abandon the process, and change the trajectory of your goals.

IF YOU BELIEVE IT,
THEN THAT IS WHAT IS TRUE.

How many times have you said to yourself something like, "It's too hard." "I can't do it." "This is impossible." "I'll never get this." Then you mentally shut down, throw your hands up, walk away, and move on to something else. Sound familiar? We've all done this at some point or another. We all get frustrated and impatient to the point that it is easier to just walk away. The defining moment, though, is if you come back to the task and try again.

The truth is, we as humans are only limited by our own insecurities and beliefs. You believe you can't do something because it is difficult. Well then, that is what is true for you because that is what you believe. We say, "I'll never get this," because in that moment of frustration and difficulty, it is what we believe to be true. Think about how liberating it would be to believe otherwise. To actually know that you can do this, that you will get this, with more work and effort. Yes, it will take time, and yes, it will take a lot of effort, energy, practice, and determination. If you accept this—and believe it—as fact, you can change your mental monologue from, "This is too hard, I'll never get this," to, "This is really hard, but I'm willing to work for it." If you really want it, then you will do the work to make it your reality.

~~I HAVE TO . . .~~ I CHOOSE TO . . .

The reality is that everything you do is a choice. Consider changing your current mindset to one that fosters self-motivation. Instead of saying, "I have to study," or "I have to practice," or "I have to do this homework assignment," get in the habit of saying, "I choose to study," "I choose to practice," and "I choose to do this homework assignment." Studying, taking a class (especially one that you're certain you probably won't even like), completing an assignment, practicing for a competition, concert, or recital—you choose to do these things or not. Yes, you probably feel pressure to complete a task on time, study for the test tomorrow, or finish the project you kept putting off, but ninety-nine percent of the time, that feeling of pressure is self-imposed, brought on by either a lack of time management, confidence, interest, or a combination of all three.

Replacing "I have to" with "I choose to" is a very powerful motivator. Controlling your outcomes is self-empowering. When you realize that you are the master of your actions, you have the ability to control the resulting outcomes and create a sense of self-efficacy. You chose to complete that assignment on time, even though you'd rather play a video game? Excellent! You didn't have to make that choice, but making that choice over what you'd truly rather do will empower and motivate you to continue to do the things you need to do to succeed in your goals. You chose to practice your instrument or your routine for the upcoming performance? Wonderful! You will be more confident, better prepared, and more successful.

You chose not to study or do that assignment? Okay, that's entirely your choice. Be prepared to be disappointed when the resulting outcome in the form of a low grade is not desirable. You chose not to take notes during class? Okay, that's fine; it is ultimately your choice to not do so. No one can make you do it. Again, do not be disappointed when you don't have what you need to complete an upcoming assignment. When the test day or the deadline comes and your teacher announces that it will be an open-note test or project, don't be mad at your teacher. How is that your teacher's fault? Your teacher enabled and empowered you with everything you needed to succeed. You chose not to take notes. Be mad at yourself for the outcome as a consequence of your choice.

Think about where you are, the current status of things in your life, and the journey that you are traversing. All of the choices that you have made over time and have had control over have led you to where you are at this moment.

In the end, knowing that you don't have to do certain things along the way but that you choose to, and therefore control your outcomes, is a powerful example of self-efficacy.

STUDY.

Such a simple word can evoke such powerful feelings of resistance and disdain. It is a word that can send even the most minimal procrastinator running for cover and looking for something, anything, to do but that. Sometimes you may even feel that doing nothing at all is better than studying. Ask yourself this question and face it head on: "Why do I hate studying so much?" Be honest with yourself. Chances are that it is one of two reasons. Studying isn't "fun." You would rather watch TV, play videogames, hang out with friends, go see a movie, or do anything else. Or you simply just don't want to study; therefore, you choose not to. Either way, you make the choice to study or not, and that choice has resulting consequences.

Studying is directly tied to the IWoWs previously mentioned—you have to work for what you want. You don't have to like it; you just have to get through it and do what you need to do to succeed and move forward. You do not have to study, but you do have to make a choice to study or not—a choice that will result in a desirable or not-so-desirable outcome. Will you stay on your path to your ultimate goal? Or will you abandon the process, accept the outcome, and change the trajectory of your goal? The choice is yours.

MORE MENTAL ENERGY,
LESS PHYSICAL ENERGY.

So often, I see students attempting to write down every single thing they hear or see. In class, students attempt to copy the teacher's slide presentation or lecture, word for word. Inevitably students will ask the teacher to go back to a slide because they didn't finish copying it. They will ask the teacher to slow down and say it again, and then again a third time. Students attempt to copy down an audio prompt, rewinding the audio six times in order to copy down every word. This constant focus on physically manipulating the source and writing down every single word is an exhaustive use and application of physical energy. Exerting this much physical energy eliminates all mental focus on what the actual content of the slides, lecture, or audio prompt is, and shifts it entirely to the physical energy necessary to manipulate the source and write down every word.

This is not how you are supposed to effectively listen, process information, or take notes. Focusing on the main details, ideas, keywords, concepts, and essential bullet points is all that is necessary at that moment. Later, when you go back to study (yes, I said *study*) and review, you can fill in any other gaps and associated information. While taking notes and writing down information does have incredible merit and value, it is much more important to mentally process the content being delivered. This is the first step towards the acquisition stage of the learning process. When you make your brain work and mentally process what you are hearing or seeing in a lecture, audio prompt, or slide presentation, you make cognitive connections between the content and your eventual output. There is more room to make mental connections and achieve acquisition when your priority is to simply listen and process than when you write and copy down words. There is so much more value to those mental connections, and it exercises the brain. A win-win.

ALMOST NOTHING WORTH DOING IS EVER EASY.

Or at least, most of the time, it seems that way. Because, when you think about it, what we're talking about in these IWoWs are typically things that we just don't want to do, but that should or need to be done. We procrastinate in doing these tasks because, well, we simply don't want to do them. They aren't fun, easy, or instant, and they require work that we don't want to put in and mental brain power that we don't want to give. It is so much easier to be mentally lazy, let it slide, and just put it away.

This is a critical moment in the trajectory of your path toward your goals. Remember that choice that we talked about earlier? This is it. If this thing that you are on the verge of choosing not to do needs to be done as a step toward the larger goal of what you want to achieve, even if you don't really want the immediate outcome of this task—honestly, you probably couldn't care less about this particular task and feel no true investment in it at all—chances are, it won't be easy for one of three main reasons: your heart isn't in it, your mind isn't in it, or the task requires more work and mental effort than you're willing to give. Admittedly, it is not an easy choice. But choosing to complete the task, stay the course, accept the challenge, and ultimately stay true to your goals, will make it worth doing. The choice is yours. Choice is a powerful thing.

ANYTHING, IF IT IS WORTH DOING, IS WORTH DOING WELL.

We're not even going to talk about the things that aren't worth doing at all. Don't waste any energy on those things, not even doing them halfway, starting them, and then abandoning them. This IWoW is for the things that need to be done, or for the things that you make a choice to do.

If you're going to do something, why would you waste your time doing it any way other than well? The old adage "do it right the first time" rings accurate and true. This includes going beyond the bare minimum by applying the DECIDE acronym described earlier and creating quality, original work rooted in integrity and honest effort.

Doing something any way other than right will result in a less-than-desirable outcome or will cause you to have to backtrack and do it again. Doing it the right way equates to doing it well—both desirable outcomes for quality work.

ALWAYS COMPORT YOURSELF AS IF SOMEONE IS LOOKING UP TO YOU. THIS WILL MAKE YOU ~~WANT TO BE~~ A BETTER PERSON.

We all have some days that are better or worse than others. Some days we feel light, carefree, and joyous, while other days, for whatever reason—sometimes for perfectly legitimate reasons and sometimes really for no reason at all—we are in a terrible mood. It happens. These particular instances are not what this IWoW is referring to.

This IWoW is about your general comportment: your bearing, the language you use, and the presence that you have in any situation or room, at any moment. You know that one kid in class who is always rude to the teacher, disruptive and talking out of turn, and thinks he's funny but he's actually super annoying? Don't be that kid. You seriously don't want that reputation, and not only because it goes against conventional classroom behavior and social norms.

Imagine that someone somewhere out there is always watching or listening to you, looking up to you, wanting to emulate you and be just like you. It could be literally anyone. It may be someone close to you, like a younger sibling, cousin, or the child of a family friend. It could be someone you don't know very well, like someone on the junior varsity team or the newest student in one of your classes. It could be someone you don't know at all and have never even met, but who is admiring you at practice, in church, on the stage, or in the cafeteria. It could be the case that there actually is someone like this out there, and you may or may not be aware. It could be just as likely that there isn't anyone at all out there who does this. The truth is, you'll probably never really know, and it honestly doesn't matter if there is or isn't. Always comport yourself in a manner that will inspire others in a positive way. This, in turn, will make you not only want to be a better person, but will actually make you a better person. You can't lose, and everyone is a better person for it.

"RUDENESS IS THE WEAK MAN'S INTERPRETATION OF STRENGTH."

—ERIC HOFFER

In the opening IWoW, nobody rises to low expectations, I mentioned that I couldn't take credit for the phrase since I heard a presenter say it in a conference I once attended. I also mentioned how profoundly this philosophy has impacted my teaching career. It seems appropriate, then, to also end this treatise with a quote that I came across many years ago. "Rudeness is the weak man's interpretation of strength." This is an overwhelmingly astute and insightful notion. Remember that rude, disruptive kid in class I talked about earlier? He thinks he's funny, a ringleader, and an influencer; he believes all that and more. The reality is, he is not any of those things. He is just not very well-behaved or well-mannered and believes that strength is shown by being rebellious and acting out of turn and outside of conventional social norms. He is misguided. The fact is that he is simply rude. (Remember, don't be that guy.)

When I discovered this quote, I printed it in large size on a full sheet of colored paper and taped it to my classroom wall. That particular year, I had a class that had some students with behavior issues, and I kid you not, when this quote went up, from that day on, the class was better behaved. I didn't even have to indicate the quote or say anything about it. It was as if the students intuitively knew the impactful truth of it and took it to heart. That was many years ago, and that same piece of colored paper is still taped to my wall.

IF IT WERE EASY, EVERYONE WOULD DO IT.

Or at least a whole lot more people than are doing it now. In life, you are constantly presented with opportunities—choices—to be the one who does it: who rises to the challenge, seeks knowledge, moves the bar, puts in the honest work, and makes progress toward achieving set goals. You can choose to learn something, do the right thing, and become a better person.

As mentioned in an earlier IWoW, nothing worth doing is ever easy. Or at least it will seem that way. There is no magical, mystical, utopian moment in life when suddenly everything is revealed and the knowledge, skills, and abilities just pour into your brain, there for your taking. These things are always there for your taking. They have always been there, and they always will be. But you have to go and get them, which requires work, determination, and a lot of choices along the way. And we return back to the beginning of these IWoWs.

I am hopeful that the Words of Wisdom presented here have helped you with the monumental task of changing your mental habits and taking the steps necessary to reset your thought processes. Even if it is only the tiniest of changes, you have begun your journey into life's ever-changing sea of choices.

Welcome to the rest of your life, day two. What choices will you make today?

ACKNOWLEDGEMENTS

Only a teacher knows how busy teachers are, how hectic their schedules are, and how little time they have for anything other than their students. With that in mind, I extend a heartfelt thanks to my friends and colleagues, Jan Jones and Karen Moody, for taking the time to proofread this little book—more than once—and for offering helpful suggestions and advice. I give extra special thanks to my good friend Vickie Watts for helping me navigate the publishing process.

Cover and back cover image by rawpixel.com.

Author photo by John Paul Lusk.

ABOUT THE AUTHOR

Amy Drossner was born into a military family in Japan, where she spent most of her childhood. She traveled extensively throughout the Far East and immersed herself in the unique characteristics and values of various cultures. She attended Florida State University, where she studied international affairs, and later, she earned an M.Ed. from Auburn University. She returned to Japan to teach English before eventually settling in Virginia to begin her teaching career at the high school and college level. After teaching for nearly thirty years, she has amassed a wealth of stories, anecdotes, and IWoWs for the younger generation.

When not doing schoolwork, Amy enjoys woodworking, crocheting, practicing music, and spending time with her family. *IWoWs* is her first publication.

Printed in the USA
CPSIA information can be obtained
at www.ICGtesting.com
LVHW020913140923
756529LV00047B/1207